# ANNE FRANK HOUSE
# in Amsterdam

Liesbeth Heenk and Marko Kassenaar

# TABLE OF CONTENTS

# INTRODUCTION

T he Anne Frank House is the most famous museum in Amsterdam. The museum attracts over a million visitors a year. A visit to the Anne Frank House, the house on Prinsengracht in Amsterdam where Anne and her family went into hiding during the Second World War, will undoubtedly have a profound emotional impact on you. The story of a young Jewish girl growing up under dangerous circumstances and writing down her innermost feelings is touching. Anne Frank has become the symbol of the Holocaust.

In this short museum guide you will read about Anne Frank and her family, the secret annexe, the daily life in the annex, the betrayal, some facts and figures about Jews in Amsterdam, the Anne Frank House, and the Anne Frank Tree. By reading it before your visit to Amsterdam you will be fully prepared.

The Anne Frank House consists of two parts. The former hiding place behind the office of Anne Frank's father is a walk-through part, refurbished in 1930s style. The modern wing houses temporary exhibitions and has a bookshop and a cafeteria. When you visit the Anne Frank House, a special route leads you from room to room. You can visit the living room, the kitchen and Anne Frank's room where you can see the pictures of art works, film stars and royals she stuck on her wall. Not all of the rooms can be visited.

Liesbeth Heenk & Marko Kassenaar

## THE FRANK FAMILY

Anne Frank was born on 12 June 1929 in Frankfurt am Main (Germany) where her father Otto Frank was a banker. The Frank Family fled to the much safer Holland after Hitler's rise to power in 1933. Otto Frank, his wife Edith and their two children Margot (1926) and Anne settled in Amsterdam where they led a happy life, and where Otto Frank became a spice merchant. Their life dramatically changed in May 1940 when the Nazi's occupied the Netherlands. Gradually the Germans denied the Jews many rights; they were no longer allowed to use public transport, they were not allowed to own a business, they had to stay inside after 8 pm. Anne and Margot had to go to an all-Jewish school, and Otto Frank had to take action to keep his own business by formally changing ownership.

On 8 July 1942 the Frank Family received a letter from the German occupiers calling up Margot Frank to a labour camp in Germany. The family did not trust the situation. To avoid deportation, they decided to carry out the plan they had been preparing for months, and moved to live secretly behind Otto Frank's company office at Prinsengracht. This hiding place was suggested to Otto Frank by his business partner Johannes Kleinmann.

Four employees, Miep Gies, Bep Voskuijl, Johannes Kleinmann and Victor Kugler, were informed that the Frank family were going to live in the annexe behind the office, and agreed to help, despite the fact that punishments were severe for helping out Jews. They did not hesitate to take on the responsibility of this risky task.

Before going into hiding they stocked up some hundred tins of food and other household products. Victor Kugler came up with the brilliant idea of the revolving bookcase which still can be seen at the museum.

## THE 'ACHTERHUIS'

C anal houses in Amsterdam sometimes had houses at the back, fully independent entities that could be reached by an alley. The Frank family moved to such an 'Achterhuis' (backhouse) of Prinsengracht 263 where Otto Frank had his businesses. Opekta sold ingredients for the manufacturing of jams and Pectacon sold spices for meat amongst others.

Shortly after they moved in, four others joined them: the Van Pels Family, father, mother and son. Hermann van Pels was one of Otto Frank's employees and an expert in herbs and spices. He was married to the elegant German lady Auguste. The last one, Miep Gies's dentist Fritz Pfeffer, originally from Berlin, joined them in November that year. Much to her annoyance, Anne had to share her room with Fritz who made odd noises while he slept. In total they were with eight people.

Anne, who always looked on the bright side of life, wrote about their hiding place: "The Annexe is an ideal place to hide in. It may be damp and lopsided, but there's probably not a more comfortable hiding place in all of Amsterdam. No, in all of Holland". She loved the sound of the bells from the nearby Westertoren they heard every 15 minutes.

The Revolving Bookcase leading to the Secret Annexe

## DAILY LIFE IN THE SECRET ANNEXE

ince the families were confined to 75 square meters, they needed a tight schedule dictated by time-slots. During the day they had to be silent as a mouse because of people in the office downstairs. Curtains had to be kept closed at all times. It was a damp and rather oppressive place to be, especially since several people smoked. Coughing, laughing or sneezing were forbidden, and all of them wore slippers to avoid making noises. Their biggest fear was getting ill and tried to keep fit by doing gymnastics during the first year into hiding. Their daily routine was scheduled around the office hours and the movements of the staff and clients downstairs; the toilet could only be flushed outside office hours.

Since the Frank family were entirely dependent on their helpers, the situation got serious when the office clerks were ill or were otherwise unable to come and bring food. There were times that they had to eat the same meal for weeks on end. Anne wrote in het diary in May 1944 that vegetables were still very hard to come by. They had to eat 'rotten boiled lettuce', and added rather sarcastically: 'Add to that rotten potatoes and you have a meal fit for a king.'

Reading and studying were the main pass time in the secret annexe. Otto Frank was an avid Charles Dickens reader and was always immersed in his novels whilst looking up words he did not know. His wife Edith was following an English language course. The quiet and studious Margot, Anne's elder sister, did a Latin correspondence course, and read various kinds of books. Anne also spent her time reading and wrote in her diary.

At 6.45 am they all got up and got ready for the day before the office downstairs opened. By the time office staff arrived at 7.30 am they were all washed and started reading and studying in total silence. During noon they could relax a bit since the warehouse workers went home for lunch. The helpers often came to see them during lunch and brought supplies. Bep brought the daily groceries, and Miep usually provided books and food. Jan Gies, Miep's husband who worked at the city of Amsterdam and was a member of the resistance, helped with ration coupons.

At 1 pm they listened to the BBC radio from London. At 9 pm everybody prepared for bed. Anne, who always wanted to look her very best, got a time slot of half an hour for her beauty routine. She would comb her hair, while wearing a special pink robe, do her nails, or bleach her moustache. Every day she wanted to look her very best. After dinner they would sometimes play a game. Sleeping for Anne was difficult at times, especially when she heard shooting. It was a challenge for the lively, outgoing Anne. Keeping a diary was her life line.

# THE BETRAYAL

An informant (the identity of whom is still unknown) betrayed them by revealing their hiding place whereupon the German *Sicherheitsdienst* in the person of Karl Silberbauer and some Dutch helpers raided the house on Friday the 4th of August 1944. After 2 years and 30 days in hiding the Frank family had been discovered and were arrested.

Otto Frank had tried to obtain visas for him and his family to get to the United States, but this had been unsuccessful. Via Westerbork, the Dutch transit camp they were all transported to Auschwitz. Edith Frank would die of exhaustion and starvation in Auschwitz in January 1945. Anne and Margot were relocated to Bergen-Belsen at the end of October 1944. Anne, aged 15, and Margot, aged 19, died of typhus in March 1945, within a few days of each other, and only weeks before the camp was to be liberated by the English troops.

Otto Frank was the only family member to survive the war. When Auschwitz was liberated by the Russian army it took him half a year to get back to Amsterdam.

"In spite of everything,
I still believe that people are good."
Anne Frank

# THE DIARIES

B efore becoming a hideaway, Anne Frank had already shown ambition to become a writer and journalist. On her thirteenth birthday Otto Frank had given his youngest daughter her first diary. She started using it in 1942 and kept writing during the years in her hiding place.

Several diaries exist. Diary 1: 12 June 1942 - 5 December 1942, Diary 2: 22 December 1943 - 17 April 1944. She probably had another diary that was used between 5 December 1942 and 22 December, but this one is lost. And her final diary, diary 3: 17 April 1944 - 1 August 1944. She transcribed her first diaries onto loose sheets which remained unfinished.

Anne describes her dreams, her fights with her parents and her emotional conflicts. Not only is the subject of her writing personal and direct, Anne Frank also shows an exceptional talent. The book is more than just a school girl writing about feelings and boys. It is literature of a promising young author with remarkable self-awareness: witty, energetic and with sharp insight into the people around her. Anne Frank planned to publish her diary as a novel after the war. The title she had in mind was 'Het Achterhuis'.

Miep Gies and Bep Voskuijl, two of the office clerks and secret helpers of the family, had found the diaries in the ransacked house and kept it safe at their homes. Eventually, they wanted to give it back to Anne in case she survived the camps. That did not happen.

Otto Frank was given Anne's diaries, and granted his daughter's wish to have them published. It appears that Anne wrote for the last time three days before the arrest. In 1947, a first edition was printed after which more editions and translations followed. In 1963, Otto Frank founded the Anne Frank Foundation, a worldwide anti-racism organisation. It took a long time before Karl Josef Silberbauer was traced which was due to Otto Frank's forgiveness.

The diaries are not the only manuscripts Anne Frank wrote. In 2004 the *Book Of Beautiful Phrases* was published. It contains fragments from books and poems Anne liked and copied. She also wrote her own poetry and *Little Stories And Events From The Annex.*

## SOME FACTS AND FIGURES

I n total some 6 million Jews were killed during the Second World War. At the outbreak of the war, an estimated 140,000 Jews were living in The Netherlands, the majority of which lived in Amsterdam. Around 100,000 of them never returned from the camps. A small proportion of the Jewish population managed to survive by going into hiding. Some two-thirds of the 25,000 Jews who went into hiding, survived.

Many books have been written about the Dutch during the war, and focus of the question how so many Jews could be deported while they looked on. Where they aware of what was going on in the camps? What did they do to prevent the deportations?

From her diary we know that Anne guessed what was going on. On 9 October 1942 she wrote about the deportations, and the rude way the Gestapo dealt with the Jews, transporting them in cattle wagons to Westerbork, the large transit camp in Drenthe. She wondered what the situation was like in the concentration camps, and was aware of gas chambers because of the daily radio broadcasts by the BBC. 'Perhaps', she writes, 'that is the quickest method of dying.'

Liesbeth Heenk & Marko Kassenaar

## HISTORY OF THE ANNE FRANK HOUSE

After the Second World War, Otto Frank continued his business and retired in 1956, and sold his office at Prinsengracht 263. The new owners planned to demolish the building. Public outrage over this plan was so fierce that it was decided to donate the building to the city. Led by Mayor Gijs van Hall, the people of Amsterdam raised funds to buy the house and surrounding buildings to be turned into a museum. In 1960, the Anne Frank House opened its doors. One of the wings of the museum was turned into a dormitory for students following summer courses in Amsterdam.

In 1997, the museum needed to expand because of the increasing number of visitors. Also, facilities had to be modernised. The students' dorms were replaced by the structure shown above. It houses the bookshop and modern exhibition spaces.

The office and hiding place were restored into their original state. The office has a brick floor like in the 1930s. The original furniture has been put back in Otto Frank's office, alongside a glass door opening onto the room of Miep Gies. In the hiding place walls are covered with copies of pictures that Anne Frank had glued on the wall herself.

## THE ANNE FRANK TREE

P ossibly the most famous tree in European history, the Anne Frank tree, was the chestnut tree that features prominently in Anne's diary. Each day, Anne would go to the attic to blow the stuffy air out of her lungs and would look out at the tree, the sky and the birds gliding on the wind. She wrote she wouldn't be unhappy – if she were to live- as long as the tree would exist with its branches and its shiny raindrops. For a moment, she would not feel like a caged bird.

This chestnut tree would become a symbol. When the borough of Amsterdam announced in 2007 that they would cut it down – it was infested with fungus - the announcement met with great resistance. The tree was so much more than a horse-chestnut tree. It was a symbol of the Holocaust. Worldwide protests, a foundation especially raised to protect the tree, and an iron structure costing € 50.000, were all to no avail. In August 2010 it was blown over in a storm. Pieces of the tree were sold for large sums of money. Eleven saplings from the tree have since been distributed amongst museums and centers across the United States.

Anne Frank is not only the symbol of the pointlessness of war and destruction. She inspires people to live their lives and exploit their talents, no matter the circumstances.

# PRACTICAL INFORMATION

For many visitors the Anne Frank House is an emotional experience. Therefore, please bear in mind that taking photographs or videos is not allowed. Moreover, the rooms and passageways are small and taking photographs will cause obstruction. Don't take a backpack or any big bag. The museum does not have a cloakroom.

There are always huge long queues in front of the museum. If you can, do book your tickets in advance! It saves your lots of time. To avoid the queue, you can book tickets online or reserve a time of arrival. You print them out, and go straight to the special entrance to the left of the main entrance. This is the most convenient way, and it saves you a lot of queuing time.

Ticket sales: http://www.annefrank.org/en/Museum/Practical-information/Online-ticket-sales/

Address: The Anne Frank House is situated in the centre of Amsterdam at Prinsengracht 263-267. It takes around 20 minutes to walk from the Central Station to the museum. Trams 13, 14 and 17 and buses 170, 172 and 174 stop nearby, at the 'Westermarkt' stop.

Do not wait until you are in Amsterdam to make the booking as the tickets sell out quickly in high season. Book them before you leave for your visit to Amsterdam.

The museum has extended opening hours in July and August: 9 am - 10 pm. During the year the museum is open 9 am -7 pm, and on Saturdays 9 am - 9 pm.

In case it is impossible to book in advance, then try to visit the museum in the evening. Last entrance: 30 minutes before closing time.

It is recommended to have a look at the Anne Frank House website because they have a great 3-D reconstruction of the annexe which gives a good idea of the rooms.

The Anne Frank House is close to Dam Square in the centre of town. Two other museums are located on this square.

**The Royal Palace** is open on a limited number of days during the year. Originally constructed as Amsterdam's town hall in the 17th century, it has beautifully decorated halls, and an exquisite collection of Empire Furniture.

The Royal Palace Amsterdam is one of the three palaces officially used by the Dutch Royal House. The Palace in Amsterdam is used for State Visits, the King's New Year receptions and many other official functions. During the period around these events the Palace is closed to the public.

**New Church** (Dutch: 'Nieuwe Kerk') next to the Royal Palace is the church where Dutch Kings and Queens are inaugurated. It houses temporary exhibitions, mostly art works from exotic cultures.

## COLOFON

Authors: Liesbeth Heenk and Marko Kassenaar

Editor: Liesbeth Heenk

info@amsterdammuseumebooks.nl

Should you wish to read more publications on Amsterdam museums, the following Kindle e-books are available from www.amsterdammuseumebooks.nl: *The New Rijksmuseum Amsterdam*, *Van Gogh Museum Amsterdam*, *The Hermitage Amsterdam*, and *Things To Do In Amsterdam: Museums*, a guide containing all four Amsterdam Museum guides.

*The New Rijksmuseum Amsterdam* by Marko Kassenaar is also available as paperback.

Made in the USA
Middletown, DE
13 December 2019